The Money Game...
and How to Win It

The Money Game...
and How to Win It

Ellen R. Abramson

Third Act Press
Ann Arbor, MI 48108
USA

Published 2019 by Third Act Press
Printed in the United States of America

20 19 18   1 2 3 4
ISBN: 978-1-7334570-0-2

This book is dedicated to David Abramson, my husband of thirty-one years. David died unexpectedly a few months after I finished writing this book. I will forever be grateful for the profound privilege it was to have had him as my life partner.
In the first fifteen chapters of this book, I tell the story of what David and I accomplished together. I added chapter sixteen shortly after he passed away.

Photo by Rose Massey

CONTENTS

Acknowledgments

Three women are responsible for guiding me down the path that led to this book. Karen Greenberg, learning of my journey paying off debt and my volunteer work helping others do the same, told me she believed my life's purpose was teaching people how to take charge of their finances. Gloria Zimet shared with me that as soon as I could give her a flyer describing my services, she was ready to refer people who wanted to learn how to manage their money. Jasna Markovac, after helping me publish my first book – *Esophageal Cancer: Real-Life Stories from Patients and Families* – said to me, "so – what's your next book going to be about? Whatever it is, I'll help you with it!" Jasna has been my editor, advisor, and teacher. She has held my hand throughout this journey. I am blessed to have these women in my life and grateful for their friendship and guidance.

Judy Ravin was at my side every day during the weeks and months after my husband died. What a deep well of kindness and generosity Judy shared with me. Without her caring and support, I question how I would have made it through the past year, let alone moved forward on this book. In addition to everything else she has done for me, Judy has been a patient reader and loving editor of the manuscript as it developed.

Debra Christein and Michael Raschke helped me believe I could eventually not only survive but thrive. Judy Kotzen reminded me of my growth over the past four decades and helped me remember what I'm capable of.

Greg Long has been at the other end of the phone nearly every week for the past year. He has listened to me process my grief and coached me as I questioned my ability to move forward in what is now required of me in my family, my business and my life. He provided support when I felt "stopped" in my writing and editing, and heartily acknowledged the successes, small and large, I was able to achieve both with the book and in my life.

Dylan Calewarts, Joe Kraut, Rose Massey, and Micah Warschausky were ardent supporters of my efforts to carve out time to work on this book. Rose switched offices with me, so I would have a quiet space in which I could concentrate. Micah answered my questions about editing documents, moving text, and tracking changes. Dylan shared his enthusiasm about the book and regularly asked about my progress. Joe's willingness to take on increased responsibility in the business allowed me the time to broaden my focus to include both the business and the book.

I am grateful beyond words to my children, son-in-law and grandchildren. You are my greatest joys, my best teachers and my most profound contributions to this world.

Finally, this story would not have existed without my dear David. What a wonderful ride we took together. I would not have missed it for anything.

Preface

This book is the story of how we paid off our debt. Many people are embarrassed by their finances. Bright, educated people feel that this is one area they cannot conquer. They turn away. They don't want to know. They believe it cannot be different.

We knew we made mistakes with money. But we were not embarrassed. We were confident that we were not the only ones. We didn't see our mistakes as proof of moral turpitude. They were just mistakes. We didn't know what we didn't know. Once we learned about money, we had a tool box. We set to work using the tools we'd acquired to rebuild the engine of our finances. It worked.

I wrote this book because I want to give people everywhere access to tools they can use to fix their finances. I want readers to feel the magnificent power that comes from being in charge of your own money.

Chapter One

The Money Game

*"I don't focus on what I'm up against. I focus on my goals
and try to ignore the rest."*
— Venus Williams

I have always been a planner. I love knowing the rules and
working creatively within them. But I never knew the rules when
it came to money. I didn't know what winning the "money game"
looked like, and I didn't know what losing it looked like.

When it came to money, I was a complete novice. Until my
husband and I began our journey, I had done only one thing right:
I had taken full advantage of the retirement savings match that
my employer offered. This decision was probably the best "one
thing right" I could have done.

In other areas of money management, I was not as successful.
Although I understood the point of a mortgage is to pay it off,

my behavior did not reflect this knowledge. Twice, when my husband and I accrued significant credit card debt, we refinanced our mortgage and incorporated the new debt. Our mortgage balance did not go down. It went up. And when we launched our business, we financed it with a home equity loan against our house.

At its height, our housing debt—mortgage and home equity loan combined—stood at $226,000. That was $103,000 more than the initial mortgage we'd secured ten years earlier. Rounding out the picture were a $36,000 recreational vehicle loan and credit card debt of nearly $20,000.

If we could pay off our debt, build savings and secure our financial future—all of which we did—so can you. This book is the story of how we did it.

I am going to show you, step by step, how you can get out of debt and build a foundation for your future. I will share the structures my husband and I created to guide our spending, saving and giving, and the mind games we played to inspire us to continue to pay down debt and build savings. All our techniques are simple, practical and ready to use.

One more thing—and this is the amazing part of our story—what we did was actually fun. It was exciting to see our debt go down and later to see our savings go up. These results empowered us, and we redoubled our efforts at this money game. We had learned the rules, we loved playing and we were on our way to winning.

Key Takeaways

- Taking charge of your finances can actually be fun.

Chapter Two

Nature Abhors a (Financial Goals) Vacuum

"If you don't know where you're going,
any road will get you there."
— Lewis Carroll

In the summer of 2008, David and I realized we were up to our eyeballs in debt. We had balances on three credit cards, a home equity line of credit (HELOC) and an RV loan. In addition to our mortgage, we were carrying $93,000 in consumer debt.

How did we get into this mess? Like many big messes, it happened little by little. David thought it started twenty years earlier when we bought a rental house to renovate. Until that time, we had never carried a credit card balance. Then we began carrying the renovation costs from month to month. We noticed that nothing catastrophic occurred. We didn't die because we had debt. Instead, we became comfortable with carrying a credit card balance.

In subsequent years, the cost of preschool for our two daughters and then private elementary school tuition made it increasingly challenging for us to make ends meet. Car repairs, house repairs and the occasional vacation were covered by the credit card as were personal growth classes and retreats. We sank further into debt.

But the most crucial factor, I believe, was that we had no financial goals. We had no north star. In the absence of a direction, we arrived at $93,000 in debt.

This is what comprised our debt at its height on August 6, 2008:

Debt	Rate	Balance
U.S. Bank VISA	8.9%	$8,668
American Express	4.99%	$4,200
American Express	3.97%	$4,900
Total Credit Card Debt		$17,768
RV Loan	7.75%	$35,690
HELOC	7.15%	$39,772
Total Debt		$93,230

We were ready to take control of our money, live within a budget and pay off our debt. But how should we start? Which debts should we pay off and in what order and how should savings fit into our plan?

To start we listed all our debts, including how much we owed on each and what the interest rate was. Then we created our goals.

We knew that having an emergency fund, even a small one, was important. So that became goal number one. Goal number two was to pay down our first card. As a reward for that success, we planned to save a bit more as goal number three and then pay down more debt as goal number four.

Specifically, our goals were:

1. Build our emergency fund to $1,000.

2. Pay down our U.S. Bank VISA balance of $8,600.

3. Build our emergency fund to $2,000.

4. Pay down our American Express balance of $4,200.

5. Pay down our American Express balance of $4,900.

6. Save $6,000 to buy a used car.

With these goals identified, we had a roadmap. We knew what winning the money game looked like for us. We knew where to put money that was in our budget and money that appeared unexpectedly. We soon found ways to free up money from other purposes to apply it to our financial goals. We loved charting our progress. It felt great to see our debt steadily decrease.

We soon realized we were charting a new course in our lives, a new course that required new behaviors. For example, I used to enjoy browsing the sales racks at Macy's and Ann Taylor. When I saw a shirt or sweater I liked, I felt I should buy it because I could use it and it was on sale.

As I stood at the Ann Taylor counter, offering the salesperson my credit card, I silently asked myself whether I had charged much on the card that month. My answer to myself was always no. I couldn't remember that I had used the card to buy anything that month. And so I moved forward with each purchase only to discover later that I had in fact charged many other items during the preceding weeks. By the time I received the credit card statement, I no longer remembered what I had bought at Ann Taylor. This lack of recall helped me realize how little the items I purchased had actually meant to me.

I thought I was doing nice things for myself. But I wasn't doing nice things for myself; I was doing nice things for Ann Taylor. And VISA. But Ann and VISA were just fine. They didn't need my help. I needed my help!

Once we had created our financial goals, I walked right past those same sales racks. I had a much bigger purpose. The pleasure of having a new shirt paled in comparison with the thrill of paying down my debt a little further. I was much closer to achieving my goals and using that money not to pay down debt, but to build wealth.

For David and me, living into our financial goals created a future that empowered us in the present. Our goals guided our choices and helped us resist ads, catalogs, commercials and the pull to keep up with others. We discovered that living into financial goals was a revolutionary way to live, one in which we defined our own success.

As we took charge of our finances, I began to create new

ledgers by which to gauge our success. Instead of being envious of a coworker's luxury car, I thought about the car payments the coworker was undoubtedly making and felt deeply grateful not to be making those payments myself. For me, no car was worth taking on debt. My perspective had radically shifted. It had become much longer range. I was looking at the end game, at what would become possible for me, my husband and our family once our debt was paid down.

When we don't have financial goals, we are sucked into the financial goals that swirl around us. We might serve Ann Taylor's financial goals. Or the goals of Macy's, Home Depot or VISA. Or the goals of a vacation club or an organization that offers seminars or personal growth classes. Buying products and services is great as long as those purchases are part of a financial plan. But when you blindly serve Macy's plan or Home Depot's plan, I believe these purchases do not serve you. David and I came to realize that living this way did not serve us.

Nature abhors a financial goals vacuum. When we have no financial goals of our own, we are continually drawn into serving the financial goals of others.

Key Takeaways

- Create financial goals (See Appendix A).

- Write them down and look at them daily.

- Keep them in mind as you make choices about how to spend your money.

Chapter Three

First Steps on the Journey from Here to There

"When eating an elephant, take one bite at a time."
— Creighton Abrams

After we created our financial goals, our next step was to create a budget. We used an Excel spreadsheet, but pencil and paper will do the job just as well. Our spreadsheet had two sections: one for income, one for expenses. We went through our checkbook register to get an idea of how much we typically spent and for what in an average month.

Categories like "Mortgage" were easiest for us to budget because the amounts did not change from month to month. Categories like "Entertainment" and "Personal" were tricky because they were a catch-all for so many purchases. These catch-all categories offered us the greatest opportunity to free up money to direct to our financial goals.

The expenses section of our budget had four columns: the category, the amount we budgeted to spend during the month in that category, how much we had actually spent in that category month-to-date and how much we had left to spend in that category for the remainder of the month. Nice, huh?

Category	Budget	Spent	Balance
Mortgage			
House Maintenance			
Debt			
Utilities			
Food			
Insurance			
Education			
Transportation			
Medical			
RV			
Savings			
Charity			
Recreation			
Personal			
Clothing			
Total			

The critical point is that the total you budget to spend each month must be equal to or less than your income for that month. Creating a way to live a wonderful life while spending less than you earn will provide you with the opportunity to create a life free of money-related stress. It will also provide you with the opportunity to build wealth.

Notice that I didn't say budgeting will provide you with the opportunity to buy lots of stuff. When David and I spent without a plan, we bought lots of stuff and in the end, all we had to show for it was debt. My husband had an "aha" moment when he realized that by using a credit card to buy a TV, dinner out or new clothing, what we were actually purchasing was debt.

Debt is a fabulously marketed product. You think you are buying one thing, but you get stuck with another.

Like lottery tickets, credit cards are expertly marketed to prey on our dreams and desires. Credit card finance charges and lottery ticket sales seem to me like a regressive tax that pulls money disproportionately from poor and middle-class people. My husband and I got sick of living that way. We decided to stop buying into the dreams offered up by our society's marketing machine. We were ready to create our own dreams.

Key Takeaways

- Build a budget that shows your income and expenses (See Appendix B).

- Use your budget every month to help you achieve your financial goals.

Chapter Four

Money Mindfulness

"If you can't measure it, you can't improve it."
— Peter Drucker

Using a spreadsheet or household budgeting program is a good way to start getting control of your finances. You will learn where the money you spent went and whether you normally break even or have money left over at the end of the month. Maybe you will discover your income is not enough for you to afford your monthly expenses.

The news may occur as good or bad. I recommend you view it as data to inform your next moves. The less meaning and drama you attach to your data, the better. In fact, reviewing your budget might also be a good time to do a little deep breathing, read any page of Eckhart Tolle's *Practicing the Power of Now* or sit quietly and empty your mind of thoughts for a few minutes. Do whatever helps you diminish your judgments.

No good can come from blaming yourself. Instead, give yourself credit for having the courage to look at your finances. For the first thirty years of my adulthood, I did a great job of not looking at my finances. Now I do a great job of looking at them. That's it. I never had the skills. No one taught me. If I had had the skills years ago, I would be in a better financial position now, but there is no sense wasting my energy feeling bad about my financial history. Instead, I feel great that I learned the skills when I did and that as soon as I had them, I ran with them. So can you.

In the first month of using our budget, I did my best to create a plan for how much we would spend in each category. Goal number one was to spend no more than we earned during the month. Goal number two was to not use credit cards at all. The last thing we needed was to add to our credit card debt.

Our first few months were all about gathering information and discovering how we actually spent our money. It was eye opening. In the first month, we discovered that we spent $511 for recreation, $434 for personal purchases and $1,010 for our home equity loan and credit-card payments. We also spent $1,261 for groceries for three people. That's $420 per person. Wow. Here is where I take few deep breaths and practice letting go of judgment.

For catch-all categories like "Personal" and "Recreation," I created additional smaller charts on each month's spreadsheet where I listed each of our expenses in that category with a formula at the bottom to add up the total. In "Recreation," we learned that we spent $54 at coffee shops. We saw how much we spent for fast food, restaurant lunches and dinners, and the *New York Times*. In "Personal," we saw how much we spent for toiletries, parking, haircuts and housecleaning. It was amazing. We were beginning to bring mindfulness to our money.

It was this mindfulness or awareness that made it possible for us to make changes. Those changes made it possible for us to dig out of debt. Digging out of debt made it possible for us to build wealth. And building wealth enabled us to pursue opportunities and experiences that otherwise would not have been accessible to us.

It all started with being willing to look.

Once the numbers were laid out in a spreadsheet, we began to manipulate them and ask ourselves questions like, "What if we were to cut this expense and move that money over here?" And, "What if we were able to free up an additional $500 per month to put toward our debt? How much sooner would we be able to pay down the first credit card?" Soon, possibilities were jumping off the page. Rather than seeing a pile of debt, we were looking at an exciting puzzle, one to which we could apply our intelligence and creativity. The process had started to become fun.

Key Takeaways

- Don't waste your energy on regret.

- Track how you spend your money.

- Look at your financial goals and spending choices and start being the boss of your money.

Chapter Five

Making Choices

"In every single thing you do, you are choosing a direction. Your life is a product of choices."
— Dr. Kathleen Hall

We quickly accomplished our first financial goal, which was to build an emergency fund of $1,000. Our second goal was to start paying down the credit card with the $8,600 balance and 8.9 percent interest rate. Of our three credit cards, this one had the largest balance and highest rate.

Many experts say you should pay down the card on which you owe the least amount of money first. That way, you experience a win as quickly as possible and that win will motivate you to move forward. This is great advice. It is advice I would give anyone who asked, but I did not follow it myself.

I didn't follow it because the 8.9 percent interest rate on our

U.S. Bank VISA card irked me. Our other cards were at 4.9 percent and 3.9 percent. We paid on time, so U.S. Bank VISA and American Express liked us very much. They also liked that we carried balances and paid interest. Every so often I called them to ask for lower rates and I was pretty successful at getting them because they knew I could transfer my balance to another card. I was picky about my balance transfers. I preferred a low rate that would not increase rather than zero interest that would bump up in a few months. I had not convinced U.S. Bank to lower that 8.9 percent any further and I had no appealing balance transfer opportunity at the time. So I decided to target that debt first.

Our strategy was to make the minimum payments on our American Express cards, RV loan and home equity loan and throw every other dollar we could at the high-balance, high-rate VISA card. To accomplish this goal, we had to free up money from elsewhere. That meant we had to commit ourselves to our budget, our blueprint, for how we would spend our money. We had to closely track our spending throughout the month to make certain we followed our plan. Mid-month adjustments were fine, but they needed to be conscious decisions, not changes that just happened and left us wondering where the money we had allocated toward debt had gone.

To create the extra money we needed to pay down our debt, we had to earn more or spend less. At the time, I had a great job as a fundraiser for medical research and education at the University of Michigan. I worked part time, which enabled me to devote attention to our younger daughter who, at fifteen years old, was still living at home. I did not want to work more hours at that point in my life. My husband worked more than full time in the business we had launched three years earlier. We decided that increasing our income in the near future was not feasible, so we launched ourselves with gusto into lowering our expenses.

First we canceled our Sunday *New York Times* subscription. For us, that was a luxury and we were no longer spending on luxuries. I started packing lunches to take to work. Going out for dinner became an occasion instead of an excuse not to cook. Starbucks became a distant memory. We were especially sad to see Starbucks go, but we loved seeing the damage the reclaimed $54 per month did to our credit card debt.

As our debt decreased, we became more energized about asking ourselves what additional changes we could make to hasten the day when we would pay off the first VISA card and move on to the other two credit cards. We made a decision to speak to the woman who had cleaned our house twice a month for a number of years. We shared with her what we were trying to accomplish and told her that for a while we would be cleaning our house ourselves. Happily for everyone, she has now been back with us for some time. But at that crucial time, the extra $150 per month made a huge difference in our pay-down trajectory.

As a result of our new choices, we shifted approximately $400 per month from new purchases to reducing credit card debt. As we paid down our debt, we started to experience how it felt to win the money game. It felt great! We had a powerful incentive to keep our expenses in control so we could continue redirecting money to debt reduction and keep feeling that great feeling of winning with money.

Fortunately we had not bought new cars for a few years and did not have to make any car payments. Instead, we drove a 1995 turquoise Ford Windstar minivan and a 1996 maroon Pontiac Sunfire. These older cars needed repairs with some regularity, but the costs weren't onerous enough to push us into buying newer vehicles on which payments would be required.

Driving our older battle-weary vehicles also afforded us a few other benefits. The cars were great for our girls to use when they learned to drive. It was easy for us to find our cars in a parking lot. We didn't need to worry about scratches or fender-benders. And that last benefit provided us with an unexpected super power whenever we were confronted by some fancy car trying to cut in front of us in line or beat us to a parking spot.

I admit I came to loathe those vehicles. Each time they broke down, I hoped the repair charge would be so high that we could not justify fixing such an old vehicle. Each time I told my daughters, "I think this could be it. We might have to get another car." And each time, time and time again, my hopes were dashed. My older daughter finally said to me, "I don't believe you when you say we might be getting a new car. Don't even bother telling me. I'll believe it when I see it."

The day finally came when we bid farewell to each of those vehicles and even though I came to hate them, I look back with fondness and appreciation for the value they provided. Our old turquoise minivan was, for me, the perfect symbol of the years we were hyper-focused on destroying our debt and laying the foundation for our future.

Key Takeaways

- Paying down debt can be fun.

- Achieving goals can make you feel powerful.

- You can put up with a crappy car if you're super-motivated to achieve your financial goals.

Chapter Six

Swimming Upstream

"Where are we headed and what are we doing in this handbasket?"
— Unknown

By now, we were excited about becoming debt-free and were constantly on the lookout for ways to reduce our spending to generate more dollars to speed up the process. We began finding money in places we had never noticed it.

For years, we kept an empty water cooler jug in the corner of our dining room and tossed loose change into it. The jug and its contents had become like wallpaper to us. Because of our passion to pay down our debt, we now saw the value of the money in that jug. Every night for a week, we put together rolls of quarters, dimes, nickels and pennies. In total, we rolled more than $400 of coins. I took the rolls to the bank, deposited them into our checking account and transferred the money to our VISA balance. Every time we made a payment, I created a new column in our debt progress chart. We loved seeing the balance decrease!

In mid-August 2008, we made a momentous decision to cash out our last mutual fund that was not retirement savings. We took that last $5,118 of liquid assets that I had inherited from my parents and applied it to the VISA card. With tremendous delight, we saw our balance drop from a whopping $8,268 to a mere $3,150.

Not long afterward, the U. S. economy fell off a cliff. Had we waited even a few weeks, our $5,118 would have been worth about $2,000. We were stunned that we had pulled out the money at just the right time.

Part of the reason we started our financial journey when we did was that we felt the rumblings and vibrations of what was coming. In our small business, we work with hundreds of radio stations. We saw more customers late on their payments. Instead of paying after thirty days, they paid after sixty or ninety. We began to receive bankruptcy notices for our customers. We had no idea the economy was going to collapse, but we knew it was headed in a bad direction. Our decision to pay down our debt with a vengeance and cash out that last account converged in a fortuitous way with the timeline of the global economic downturn.

We were grateful that our finances were no longer a mystery to us. We knew where every dollar went. In fact, we were actively directing where every dollar went. This knowledge positioned us to determine where to cut further in our monthly budget. As financial institutions collapsed, stores closed on our Main Street and people we knew lost their jobs, we continued to slowly and steadily pay down our debt.

In January 2009, five months into our new way of living, we made our last payment of $400 to our 8.9 percent VISA card. Our total credit card debt was now $8,302, down from $17,768. We were energized, excited and ready to keep going.

As the economy settled into its deep and terrifying trough, we tackled the next debt on our list. Six months later, in July 2009, it was paid off. In March 2011, as the economy was about to enter its next awful dive, we paid off the last penny of our $17,768 credit card debt.

Debt	Rate	8/6/2008 Balance	1/31/2009 Balance	7/30/2009 Balance	3/31/2011 Balance
U.S. Bank VISA	8.90%	$8,668	$0	$0	$0
American Express	4.99%	$4,200	$3,800	$0	$0
American Express	3.97%	$4,900	$4,502	$4,065	$0
Total Credit Card Debt		$17,768	$8,302	$4,065	$0
RV Loan	7.75%	$35,690	$34,850	$34,084	$31,396
HELOC	7.15%	$39,772	$37,664	$35,462	$27,500
Total Debt		$93,230	$80,816	$73,611	$58,896

Key Takeaways

- Have a plan.

- Follow your plan.

- Keep a debt progress chart (See Appendix C).

- Be the boss of your money.

Chapter Seven
Eye of the Storm

"If you're going through hell, keep going."
— Winston Churchill

As I look back at our financial journey, I am gripped by terror by the part of it that should have been the most boring: our mortgage. Here, in our tale of refinancing and loss of equity, resides the eye of the financial storm through which many Americans walked. I am grateful that at the time, I didn't know enough to be afraid.

We purchased our home in 1998 for $197,000. At that time, we secured a thirty-year mortgage of $123,000 with a fixed interest rate of 7.375 percent. We had a gain on the sale of our first home, and that provided the substantial down payment for our second. We had a nice mortgage and had made a great down payment. It was a solid situation.

Five years later, as the subprime securities market boomed and mortgage rates plummeted, the market value of our home soared to $328,000, an increase of $131,000—or more than 60 percent—in five years. We heard no alarm bells ringing. We along with our fellow citizens were living in some sort of nationwide delusion, and too thrilled at our good fortune to be concerned about the future.

In June 2003, we replaced our original mortgage with a new thirty-year fixed-rate mortgage at 5.625 percent. While refinancing, we borrowed an additional $80,000. Our mortgage now stood at $203,000.

Looking back, it is remarkable to me how glibly we entered into an additional $80,000 of debt. Worse yet, I have no clear memory of how we spent the money. A lot of it likely went to pay credit card debt. Around that time, my husband and I participated heavily in personal growth classes and retreats. Many of these experiences were deeply valuable, but since we routinely charged them to our credit cards, they added significantly to that debt.

People tell me they don't use a budget because they cannot bear the thought of denying themselves the things and experiences they desire. When I think back to this time in our lives, when my husband and I spent money with abandon and dug ourselves deeply into debt, I wonder how our lives would have been different if we had lived with financial goals and a plan to achieve them.

A part of me is grateful for the recklessness that allowed us to take the classes and workshops. But I also believe that if we had understood the power of financial goals, we would have found ways to strike a balance between personal growth and a strong financial foundation. After all, both goals were important to our family and our future. A commitment to a strong financial foundation required a longer perspective.

What I know now is that it is possible to take actions to achieve long-term goals while at the same time ensuring we have meaningful and enjoyable experiences today. Looking back, I have no regrets. But had we known then what we know now, I believe we would have made different choices—ones that could have brought us the joy of personal growth without the millstone of debt.

When we woke up to our finances in the summer of 2008, the market value of our home had dropped to $240,000. It was still worth more than when we purchased it in 1998, but because we had increased our housing debt considerably, the equity in our home now stood at a mere $14,000. We owed $226,000 and our equity was less than 6 percent of our home's value. On the day we purchased our home in 1998, our equity was nearly 38 percent! I am still astounded by the impact of our poor financial decisions.

Compounding our loss of home equity was the fact that the line of credit we had obtained for our business was secured against the value of our house. The limit on our home equity line of credit had been reduced to the exact amount we owed so there was no possibility of pulling more money out of our house. Had our business cash flow imploded, we could have lost our home. And, in terrifying hindsight, the U.S. economy was just months away from its deepest recession since 1929.

At the time, I did not panic. I kept my head down, worked hard at my job and started paying off credit card debt. My husband seemed better able to grasp the gravity of our situation. He was hit hard by the letter from Chase Bank that said they were lowering our home equity line to the precise amount we owed at that time. I am not certain he realized we were at risk of losing our home. But I am certain he understood that our last financial lifeline had been cut. We were on our own.

David worked like a madman selling, selling, selling and leading our small sales team in selling, selling, selling. Meanwhile, I worked on reducing our business expenses. We bailed out the proverbial boat as fast as we could, managing to stay afloat.

But the stress took a toll on David. He ended up in the hospital emergency room with symptoms that felt like a heart attack. Fortunately, he had an esophageal spasm and not a heart attack; however, tests revealed underlying heart issues which did turn out to be a major issue in our future.

I survived the stress by compartmentalizing our business and personal finances. With our personal finances, we were steadily paying down debt. We had a sense of control, and it felt like we were winning. With our business finances, we were doing our best. We determined on a weekly basis which bills we could pay and which we couldn't. David had frequent conversations with our vendors, keeping them apprised of what we could pay and when. We created a more effective process to track our receivables and secure payment from our customers, many of whom were struggling financially. We stayed afloat and looked to the future.

Key Takeaway

- Keep working your plan.

Chapter Eight

The Big One

*"I am not someone who is ashamed of my past. I'm
actually really proud. I know I made a lot of mistakes, but
they, in turn, were my life lessons."*
—Drew Barrymore

Once you decide to take charge of your finances, your starting point is wherever you are. You might wish your finances looked different. You might regret financial choices you made in the past. You might look with envy at other people's financial situations. But you are where you are, and that is your starting point. Your mistakes will provide you with your greatest lessons. This chapter is about one of our biggest mistakes and the lessons we learned from it.

In August 2007, David and I bought a thirty-one-foot class C motorhome with a kitchenette, bathroom and sleeping accommodations for six people. This RV cost $38,801. We made a down payment of $2,000 and financed the rest with a fifteen-year mortgage at 7.75 percent. Had we owned the RV for the full life of the mortgage, we would have paid finance charges totaling $25,563. The all-in cost of that $38,801 RV would have been $64,365.

I still cannot believe we bought it, and the expense didn't stop with the purchase. The navigation system cost $1,107 and insurance was about $900 annually. There were also routine maintenance costs and fees to park in RV campgrounds. For a number of years, we paid $55 per month to keep the RV in storage. The few times we actually drove it, one gallon of gas took us only about ten miles down the road.

On July 11, 2012, we sold the RV for $6,000 less than we owed on it and although it was painful to pull the $6,000 from our emergency fund it was a great relief to get the RV debt off our balance sheet. In all, David and I had probably driven the RV a total of five times, no more than ten days, in the five years we owned it. We paid about $38,000 for those ten days.

How did this happen to us? Looking back, I realize there were multiple factors.

First, we looked at how much we could supposedly afford, rather than at the actual cost. The monthly payment of $346.47 appeared doable and I am sure the nice salesman at the motorhome dealership went over the fine print with us. I am sure he pointed out the finance charge, interest rate and total cost, including interest. I don't remember whether we also met with someone from the bank. If we did, I am sure that person also would have pointed out the finance charge, interest rate and total cost with interest.

But it made no difference to us because we had no bigger

context, no financial goals. We wanted our business to be a success and we wanted to be able to pay our bills. That was it. Or, to be totally honest, we didn't actually care about being able to pay our bills. We were happy to use credit cards. There was no reason for us to think strategically about our finances or put any real thought into the step we were about to take in buying the RV.

Second, my husband and I were not working as a team. Before he met me, David had owned a small camper in which he sometimes lived for months at a time. He missed that lifestyle and the freedom he had. Our family came up with the idea of our buying a motorhome. They had fun researching it and finding one that looked good to them. David got caught up in the excitement of it.

Mine was a very small voice saying, "I don't think this RV is a good idea." I had never spent any time in an RV. I had no fond memories of camping or traveling in one. But I loved my husband, I knew he worked hard and I thought he deserved some rewards for his hard work.

We had no financial knowledge and no financial advisor. My parents, who might have offered a voice of reason, had passed away. No one, including us, was looking at our bigger picture and thinking about whether an RV would work for or against us getting to where we wanted to be in our lives. With no larger perspective to guide us, all systems were GO and we signed on the dotted line.

When we woke up and began to take charge of our finances in August 2008, we realized we had RV debt of $35,690. At the time, our business had taken on a lot of debt and we were busy bailing out the boat there. Meanwhile, we felt empowered about paying down our credit card debt. Those were the areas where we put our focus.

It was hard for us to look at the RV debt and we didn't know how to handle it. My husband was fond of saying, "Nobody out there is stupid enough to buy our RV!" But I knew different. I told him, "Yes, there are people stupid enough to buy our RV. I know that because we were stupid enough to buy it." I also hoped there were people for whom our RV would not be a stupid purchase. Maybe they were retiring and downsizing from a bigger home or perhaps they wanted to live near their children for half of the year and our RV would provide them with an affordable way to do that. I hoped for a positive outcome for all.

We set a goal to sell our RV by August 2011. I reached out to the nice man who had sold us the RV from his dealership in 2007. We handed our RV over to him, so he could do some cosmetic repairs and begin to show it. In early 2012, he reported that he had an interested buyer, but the buyer already owned an RV and owed more than it was worth, so that potential sale was unlikely to move forward. Spring RV shows offered hope since many people who attend experience sticker shock and decide to buy a used RV instead of a new one. We were well-positioned for that market.

In May 2012, the dealer advised us to lower our asking price from $30,000 to $27,000. Since we had agreed he would earn $4,000 for the sale, this price cut would lower our net from $26,000 to $23,000. At the time, we still owed about $29,000 on the RV. With eyes wide open, we agreed to lower the price.

On July 11, 2012, we were free of the RV. We signed over the title and paid Citizens Bank $6,337.29. The nice man who owned the dealership made money when we bought our RV and when we sold it. Good for him.

We also benefited in the sense that we learned valuable lessons. We learned that we could have rented an RV for a week rather than buying one. We learned that the true cost of financing a four-year-old class C motorhome for fifteen years is $64,000, not $38,000. We learned that if something is valuable to you, it makes more financial sense to save for it and pay cash or mostly cash. If it doesn't mean enough to you to save for it and pay cash, then it certainly doesn't make sense to pay an additional $26,000 in interest to finance the purchase of it.

At this point in our financial journey, we had not thought much about opportunity costs. If we had, we would have been motivated to sell our RV much sooner. In an average month, we were paying $346 for the RV loan, $75 for insurance and $55 for storage, a total of $476. Had we invested that sum, even at 1 percent, we would have had $92,000 at the end of fifteen years. With a growth rate of 5 percent, we would have had $127,000 at the end of fifteen years. That was our opportunity cost.

The good thing about hard lessons, like the lesson of opportunity cost, is that we can share them with others. Our children and friends—and you—can benefit from our experience. You can see where the sand traps are, and you can avoid them.

And so, we sold our RV, dusted ourselves off and kept moving forward. With the sale, our balance sheet shed $29,000 of debt and we only lost $6,000 of savings. We were $23,000 to the good. Here is what our debt looked like at the end of July 2012:

Debt	Rate	7/31/2012 Balance
U.S. Bank VISA	8.90%	$0
American Express	4.99%	$0
American Express	3.97%	$0
Total Credit Card Debt		$0
RV Loan	7.75%	$0
Auto Loan	3.49%	$4,082
HELOC	7.15%	$16,722
Total Debt		$20,804

Key takeaways

- From our mistakes we learn our greatest lessons.

- Learn from your mistakes.

- Learn from other people's mistakes.

- Cut your losses.

Chapter Nine

The Journey Continues

"I am an optimist. It does not seem too
much use being anything else."
—Winston Churchill

Selling the RV was a huge psychological turning point for us. We were released from what had felt like a millstone around our necks. In the wake of that big 'win', our enthusiasm to continue our journey of fixing our finances and winning the money game grew even stronger.

Though we paid off all our credit card debt and unloaded the RV, we had also chosen to take on a new debt. In March 2011, our 1995 Ford Windstar minivan was at death's door, and I was at the end of my rope at the thought of driving it any longer, so we bought a newer used car, a 2007 Honda Accord with 80,000 miles on the odometer. I was thrilled to be driving what felt to me like a brand-new car.

We had saved $7,000 toward the purchase of a car and the Honda cost $10,500, so we needed to borrow $3,500. The University of Michigan Credit Union was willing to provide a loan for the full cost at 3.49 percent. Although we were allergic to taking on new debt, the car loan's interest rate was half the 7.15 percent we were paying for our home equity loan, so it was too good to pass up.

Given this situation, we came up with a sort of debt compromise. We borrowed $7,000 from the credit union, used $3,500 toward the purchase of the car and used the other $3,500 to take a chunk out of our higher interest home equity loan.

Debt	Rate	2/28/11 Balance	3/31/11 Balance	7/31/2012 Balance
U.S. Bank VISA	8.90%	$0	$0	$0
American Express	4.99%	$0	$0	$0
American Express	3.97%	$2,006	$0	$0
Total Credit Card Debt		$2,006	$0	$0
RV Loan	7.75%	$31,561	$31,396	$0
Auto Loan	3.49%	$0	$7,000	$4,082
HELOC	7.15%	$27,994	$24,000	$16,722
Total Debt		$61,561	$62,396	$20,804

Other than our primary mortgage, our home equity loan was our last remaining big debt. We decided that if we could get a low rate, it might make sense for us to refinance one last time and roll our home equity loan into a new first mortgage. After several failed overtures to mortgage loan officers between 2008 and 2012, we were finally eligible to refinance in August 2012, when our equity reached 22 percent.

We were determined to make good choices with this refinance. We lowered our interest rate from 5.625 percent to 3.375 percent, and we shortened our term by replacing the thirty-year mortgage we had assumed in 2003, which had twenty-two years left on it, with a fifteen-year mortgage that would end seven years sooner.

In late 2012, credit card debt made a brief reappearance. In August 2012, our older daughter married a wonderful young man. We began planning for a wedding sometime earlier and had managed to save nearly $18,000. However, when expenses exceeded our budget by about $2,500, we put the balance on the VISA. We were determined that our first order of business would be to pay it off. Two months later the VISA balance was back to zero.

By December 2012, we could have paid off the car loan, which was our last short-term debt. But I delayed making the final payment. For four years, we had been laser-focused on paying down debt. It was a great game, and we had gotten really good at it. It was hard for me to complete the game without having another to play. I needed a new set of goals to motivate me and a reason to continue being mindful with our money.

David couldn't wait to be free of the car loan, and his excitement was the motivation I needed. In May 2013, we had the glorious experience of providing a check for $2,759 to the University of Michigan Credit Union, making the final payment on our last short-term debt.

		10/31/12	5/31/13
Debt	Rate	Balance	Balance
Auto Loan	3.49%	$3,645	$0
HELOC	7.15%	$0	$0
U.S. Bank VISA	8.90%	$0	$0
Total Debt		$3,645	$0

Paying off our debt took nearly five years. We had begun our journey in August 2008 with short-term debt totaling more than $93,000. In May 2013, we achieved our goal of paying off every penny of it.

It was time to start dreaming. What did we want to create now that our money wasn't being used to pay down debt? How did we want our lives to look? And what financial goals would help us get there?

Key Takeaways

- It is possible to pay off debt.

- Setting realistic goals and working your plan is how you do it.

Chapter Ten
Top of the Balance Sheet

"Ambition is the path to success. Persistence
is the vehicle you arrive in."
— Bill Bradley

The summer of 2012 put us into a whole new phase of taking charge of our money. The big debts were handled and it was time to start socking money away. Cash, which had been going to pay down debt, was freed up to build savings.

By May 2013, the month in which we made our last car loan payment, we had already built an emergency fund of more than $10,000. We now created a goal to build a fully funded emergency fund, one that would cover three-to-six months of household expenses. Our monthly overhead was about $5,000, so we decided to shoot for three months of expenses, a $15,000 savings goal.

When we began to take charge of our money in 2008, I was

working 60 percent of full time at my job at the University of Michigan. In the first half of 2011, I increased my hours to 70 percent. With a daughter still in high school, I wanted to be available after school and have the flexibility to be involved in school activities. Even with the increase in work time, I was able to do that.

When my daughter graduated in June 2011, I did not need to be as available to her, and eighteen months later, in December 2012, I increased my work hours to full time. With the increased revenue from my full-time employment, no money going toward debt payments and the continued discipline of using a monthly budget, we quickly reached our emergency fund savings goal.

Savings	8/31/12	5/31/13	12/31/13
Emergency	$775	$10,985	$15,131
College	$3,860	$2,420	$1,180
Insurance	$240	$393	$875
Total Savings	$4,875	$13,798	$17,186

The Insurance savings category shown in the chart was really a "sinking fund" (See Appendix D). When we began budgeting in 2008, we started the practice of adding up all the insurance payments (for life, disability, long-term care, and car insurance) which would be due throughout the year. We divided the total by twelve and this was the amount we saved each month. As a result, we were confident that when these bills came due, we would have the money to pay them. This brought us tremendous peace of mind. I remember with discomfort the dread we used to experience when the insurance bills arrived, before we took on this savings practice.

Now let's talk about college savings. When our two daughters were in elementary school, we opened college savings plans for them. Amazingly, even though we were very poor savers, each girl had about $12,000 in her account by the time she reached college age.

Our older daughter started living an Orthodox Jewish lifestyle at age 14, taking on a level of observance far beyond that of the rest of our family. She had spent time with our local Lubavitch Chassidic (a type of observant Judaism) community, and the way they looked at the world spoke to her heart and soul. Throughout high school, she became increasingly determined to anchor her life within this community.

Though a traditional college education was not a priority for her, she wanted to attend a year of training at a teachers' seminary in Israel. Because the seminary had a connection with a college in the United States, we were able to use her college savings funds to pay for a substantial portion of her year of study. When she returned to the United States, she pursued an additional year of post-secondary education, the cost of which we included in our monthly budget.

Our younger daughter attended Michigan State University, which cost about $20,000 per year, including room and board. For the first three years, we used about $4,000 of her college savings, or about one-third of the total, per year. Another $4,000 came from our daughter working for our family business, and we paid the remaining $12,000 from our monthly income. In her fourth year, a reduced course load, living off campus and her income from several part-time jobs helped make ends meet. We incorporated the remaining costs into our monthly budget. In some months, the money we budgeted was paid directly to the university. In other months, the money went into a savings account until it was due to be paid. In February 2015, we made our final payment to Michigan State University.

With college paid for and our emergency fund built, we shifted our focus to the next big goal—the "Freedom Fund." That category was a whole other story.

Key Takeaways

- Keep a savings progress chart (See Appendix E).

- You can achieve goals faster when you're bringing in more money.

- You can achieve savings goals faster when your money isn't going to pay down debt.

- Everything works better when you have a plan.

Chapter Eleven

The Freedom Fund

"If you live like no one else, later you can
LIVE like no one else."
—Dave Ramsey

When I increased my work hours to full time and took on new job responsibilities in November 2012, I knew I would face a steep learning curve and high expectations. As a major gift officer for the University of Michigan Health System, I was tasked with raising at least $2 million annually in new charitable commitments benefitting medical research and education. For the fiscal year that ended June 2013 and two of the next three fiscal years, I substantially exceeded that metric. I was doing well and earning a good income, but the stress I felt due to repeated organizational restructurings and leadership changes and starting each year at zero, wondering how I would reach the $2 million mark, was wearing on me.

I experienced months of restless nights and stress-filled days during our first organizational restructuring. At times, it was unclear to me to whom I reported or which departments I served and even whether I would be able to retain my job. I worried about the toll this stress might be taking on my health.

A number of years earlier, I had returned to the university after a hiatus of five years during which I worked for the American Red Cross. Upon my return, I learned that I could regain credit for my earlier twelve years of service once I had been back for ten years. In other words, I would receive credit for my earlier twelve years of service on my subsequent ten-year anniversary date. It is always a good idea to ask about these sorts of things if you leave an employer and later return.

After the ten-year anniversary of my second stint at U-M, my combined twenty-two years of service along with my age would make me eligible to retire with benefits. The most valuable benefit and most compelling reason to reach the ten-year milestone was that the university would then pay the majority of David's and my health insurance premiums for the rest of our lives. That's a pretty great benefit. There was no way I would leave my job before June 21, 2014.

There was, however, a fly in the ointment. For employees hired prior to 1988, health insurance benefits began immediately upon retirement regardless of the retiree's age. For those hired in 1988 or after, health insurance benefits would not begin until age 62. My original date of hire would have made me eligible for the enhanced benefit, but because I left the university for a time, my service date became the date of my return, which was June 21, 2004. If I retired in June 2014, I would be 57 years old and we would have to pay 100 percent of our health insurance premiums until I turned 62. I avoided taking a hard look at what that would mean for our finances and continued to dream about retiring in 2014.

When we finally met with our retirement savings advisor and did the math on the health insurance premiums, I decided it was in the best interest of our financial future for me to work through 2015. I also decided that I could not retire responsibly until we had saved the money needed to cover what we would owe in health insurance premiums for the three-plus years before the university benefit kicked in. That savings goal became known as my "Freedom Fund."

I gave this savings goal that name because the money would enable me to free myself from working for someone else. Once the goal was achieved, I would be able to immerse myself in the business my husband and I owned. I also dreamed of starting a consulting practice to help people learn how to take charge of their money, and having the time to learn new skills and explore new interests. In other words, I would be the master of my own time. It was a fabulous, exciting, empowering goal.

In December 2015, we reached our "Freedom Fund" goal. I worked part time for a few more months while the university searched for my successor. On April 15, 2016, I retired from the University of Michigan.

My "second act" had begun!

Key takeaways

- Be willing to look at what it will take to achieve your goals.

- Keep working your plan.

Chapter Twelve

Giving Money Away

"Giving opens the way for receiving."
—Florence Scovill Shinn

David and I had always supported nonprofit organizations that we believed in, but it wasn't until we started budgeting and working toward achieving specific financial goals that we began doing so in a consistent and mindful way.

We referred to our donations as *tzedakah*, a Hebrew word that, in its closest translation into English, is a cross between justice and charity. The idea of *tzedakah* is that we are obligated to use a portion of our income to help others. *Tzedakah* is based on a belief that a portion of our income has never actually belonged to us. For that portion, we are merely stewards, directing it to where we believe it will do good.

Tzedakah was part of our first budget in August 2008. Over the years, as we paid down debt, we increased the *tzedakah* line item of our budget. Normally, we would spend the full amount during a single month, but sometimes we would carry over part of it to the next month.

The funny thing about *tzedakah* is that when you know you have budgeted an amount of money to donate each month—even when it is a relatively small amount—it gives you an expansive feeling. You know you have enough to help others as well as care for yourself. You see you have a critical role in the care of your community and the healing of the world. You understand that you make a difference.

Tzedakah is a blessing not only to those who receive it. It also blesses those who give it.

Key Takeaway

- Include charitable giving in your monthly budget.

Chapter Thirteen
Time - Money - Meaning

"We are our choices."
—Jean-Paul Sartre

As I got closer to leaving my job at the university, I had second thoughts.

David and I were out of debt and done paying for college. Our business was starting to make a profit and I was earning a great salary. I began to wonder whether I was crazy to leave a job with a great salary and benefits. With nothing holding us back, we could really be socking away money!

My next thought was: Socking away money for what? We were still driving our 2007 Honda and another used car and had no aspirations for newer fancier vehicles. We had no big consumer product aspirations. Thanks to years of saving, supplemented by a generous match from the University of Michigan, for which I will be forever grateful, we were in good shape with retirement savings. Other than for travel and other learning and growing experiences, why did we need to amass money?

I also found myself thinking about my parents, both of whom passed away when I was in my twenties. My mom died at age 66, my father at age 68. Both my parents lived with chronic illness much of their adult lives. I had just celebrated my fifty-eighth birthday. I didn't think my parents' path would be my path. However, I thought it was a good idea to be informed by their experience. We don't know when we will die, but we do know that our time is limited.

So I began to think about the limited resource of time and the potentially unlimited resource of money. I found myself balancing the two resources in my mind: time-money, time-money, time-money. It didn't take long for me to decide that time was the clear winner for me. I made my decision to retire and shared it with my supervisor and the heads of the medical departments I served.

The decision felt right to me. I was energized and excited about the future, but my husband had concerns about me stepping down from my job. It was hard for him to believe we would be okay financially without my salary. Even when I showed him we had been putting the majority of my paycheck into savings each month for nearly a year, he fought against the grip of an old fear: he had grown up poor and didn't want to feel poor again.

Without my salary, we would be relying entirely on our family business to support us. We had launched the business in 2005 and weathered the serious storm of the Great Recession in 2008 and 2009. As we saw businesses closing their doors and members of our community losing their jobs, we said to ourselves, "We can't be sure we'll always be able to pay ourselves, but we can be sure that our own actions will have a lot of impact on whether we can." There was a myriad of actions we could take to influence our revenue and expenses and keep our business moving forward. In other words, we had some control over our destiny. We knew my retiring from the university posed a risk. But it was a calculated risk and we were ready to take it.

For many years, there had been a positive interplay between our business and my employment. Had I not worked for the university and brought home the benefits, we might never have taken the risk to launch the business. Had we not had the business for me to step into, I might not have considered leaving my job.

For many years, I had worked for the university during the day and managed our business's finances in the evenings and on weekends. Taking on a leadership role in our business had become a dream of mine and now I would be able to move in that direction. My husband, who had steered the ship for many years, was thrilled at the prospect of spending less time running the business and more time coaching community leaders and entrepreneurs and volunteering with a nonprofit he had helped found.

After I left the university, I realized there was another dimension to my time-and-money consideration. This third dimension had been there the whole time, hiding in my blind spot. What I was really struggling with was balancing time, money and meaning. I used to try to fit activities that were meaningful to me into my life when I was exhausted after work or between chores on the weekend. After I left my job, those activities became part of what I did every day. I am in charge of my time and able to focus on what gives my life joy and meaning.

David and I were both launching our "second acts." We were engaged in exciting new challenges and meaningful community projects. We had the time and scheduling flexibility to exercise, prepare great meals, take classes and learn new skills. We fulfilled a long-held dream of taking our children and grandchildren on a trip to Jerusalem.

For all this, I was—and am—deeply grateful.

Being able to do the things that really matter to you.....this, I believe, is the payoff for taking charge of one's finances. It is the reason to use a monthly budget and the purpose behind paying off debt and building savings. A budget helps you make choices today that make magic possible tomorrow.

Key Takeaways:

- Create dreams that inspire you.

- Take calculated risks.

- Determine what's important to you.

- Be courageous.

Chapter Fourteen
Miracles

"Miracles happen every day; change your perception of what a miracle is and you'll see them all around you."
—Jon Bon Jovi

During the nearly five years it took David and me to pay off our debt, we employed a lot of strategies. We learned that when you want to pay down debt, build savings and achieve financial goals, there are three ways to do it. You can spend less, bring in more or do both. Spending less is all about math. Bringing in more begins to move into miracle territory.

I thought it was a miracle that we cashed out our last $5,118 in mutual funds to pay down our credit card debt just weeks before the economy crashed and the money would have lost 60 percent of its value. Bundling the coins in our water jug and paying down $400 of credit card debt also felt miraculous.

It was a miracle when I discovered I was owed approximately $1,200 in back pay by my employer. Another work-related miracle came in the form of $600 in rewards I earned for recommending several potential new employees who were eventually hired. Smaller miracles were holiday gift cards I received from my employer, sometimes from a number of different departments and often totaling $150 or more.

Speaking of gift cards, once we got serious about paying down debt, we went through our junk drawers and found a bunch of them. Gift cards enabled us to buy extras that were not in our budget, like a Ninja blender and set of new Cuisinart stainless steel cookware.

Another big miracle happened when my boss agreed to increase my work hours from 60 percent of full time to 70 percent. My hours increased in August 2011, one month before my daughter entered college. The timing was perfect.

The next big miracle came the following year when the health system development operation was reorganized. Before the reorganization, I worked on alumni outreach, annual fundraising campaigns and major gift fundraising for the Department of Orthopaedic Surgery. After the reorganization, I had just one responsibility—major gift fundraising—for several departments. I didn't know whether I would be successful, but it seemed to me that working full-time would give me a better chance of success. When I requested an increase to full-time employment, my new boss was thrilled. My income increased substantially.

My friends created money miracles, too. One wanted to visit her son who had moved to California. She had not budgeted for this trip and did not want to take on debt to pay for it. She was part of our "Prosperity Year" initiative – a group of friends who met once a month to learn and share about creating and achieving personal and financial goals. She had heard there were jewelry stores in town that paid cash for unwanted gold jewelry. An idea was born! She sold a necklace and bracelet she no longer wanted for $1,200. That money made her trip possible.

Members of our group researched unclaimed property websites for the State of Michigan and other states where they had lived. Several regained their unclaimed assets ranging from six dollars to more than $1,000. One regained $538, of which $150 was a refund from Sprint and the other $388 was from an old Primerica account. Another reclaimed $700 of corporate stock left to her by her grandmother from the unclaimed property division of the State of New York.

Recently I have been working my way through each room of my home, cabinet by cabinet, drawer by drawer, and removing items I no longer need or want. Most are donated, others thrown out or recycled. A former colleague told me she sold a dining room set and other items through a local high-end thrift shop. When the shop sold her item, she received 65 percent of the sale price. I took a pile of stuff to the shop and paid the $15 annual membership fee. The women in the intake area researched my items on their databases and priced my vintage Coca-Cola crate at $25 and a set of pewter goblets at $12. Two small metal trays were priced at $6 each. Another tray, to my surprise, turned out to be sterling silver and was priced at $75. Three months later, I received a check for $73. A second pile of stuff brought me another $40. More donations and consignment transactions followed as I continued to find items in my home that I no longer used or enjoyed.

Are these miracles? That depends on your definition of a miracle. Because I looked and listened, I saw opportunities I otherwise would have missed and I acted on them. My miracles and my friends' miracles were part mindset, part action and part good fortune.

Key Takeaways:

- Choose to see miracles.

- Notice when the universe aligns to help you achieve your goals.

Chapter Fifteen
Don't Go In There Alone

"You can never solve a problem on the level
on which it was created."
—Albert Einstein

Have you ever noticed that it is hard to keep a commitment you make only to yourself? If no one knows you have made a commitment, it is easy to forget about it. If everyone knows (e.g., because you've posted it on social media), it is still like no one knows. You have empowered no one to hold you accountable.

The very best tool my husband and I had in paying down our debt and building our savings was each other. Believe it or not, it was fun for us to work together on being disciplined with our finances. Once we stopped at a Starbucks just so my husband could walk inside and inhale the coffee aroma. Then he came back to the car and we were on our way. No money spent!

We sometimes played a game we called "Abundance on a Shoestring." The objective was to figure out how we could have a good time without spending money. Because we lived in a university town, it was not hard to find free things to do. Occasionally, we hosted "Abundance on a Shoestring" parties. Everyone was asked to bring a potluck dish and some sort of self-expression such as a poem, song, story or artwork to share with the group. Those were amazing gatherings.

When it comes to budgets and projects, I am especially good at managing details. My husband was not always great at details, but he saw trends and opportunities in the big picture that I could miss. Together, we were much more effective than we would have been acting individually. We were also fortunate in that we rarely disagreed about financial goals and priorities. Our values were in alignment.

Together, we received a very solid grounding in financial goals and how to achieve them through Dave Ramsey's *Financial Peace University*. In this course, Ramsey lays out key financial goals and the order in which to tackle them. With this shared knowledge, it was easy for my husband and me to work together.

I built our budget at the beginning of each month and we worked together carrying out the plan. During our intense years of paying down debt, I printed an updated budget each week showing our expenditures to date and budgeted funds remaining in each category and taped it to our bathroom mirror. That way, David saw where we stood and how much money was left for the month.

When we paid down our debt and moved into our savings phase, David suggested I add a small chart to our budget spreadsheet that showed where we stood on our savings goals with numbers for the previous and current months. That was a great addition and it kept us focused on our targets.

If you don't have a spouse or life partner, connect with a friend who is committed to transforming his or her finances. Become accountability buddies. Share where you are with your finances. Develop your top-priority financial goals and share them with each other. Meet once a month to do a spot-check of each other's budgets. Celebrate each other's successes and remind one another to take the long view when you experience setbacks. People who talk about their financial goals are much more likely to achieve them.

Work with a coach who can help you develop specific, actionable financial goals and build a monthly budget to support your efforts to achieve them. Your local credit union may offer budget counseling at no charge or you can hire a private consultant.

A few years ago, I launched a consulting practice, Money Mindfulness, LLC, to assist people who are ready to take charge of their finances. A second set of eyes, broader perspective and experience can add remarkable value when you begin the journey of becoming the boss of your money. More information about my consulting services can be found at the end of this book.

Key Takeaways

- Achieving financial goals is a big game. Play it with a partner.

- If you don't have a life partner, find someone who's interested in achieving his or her own financial goals. (Hint: everyone is interested in achieving their own financial goals.)

- Support one another.

Chapter Sixteen

Life Insurance

"Welcome to a new day of loving."
—David Abramson

David and I were married for thirty-one years. We were life partners for nearly thirty-six. He passed away at age 63, just nine days after my sixtieth birthday. David's death was unexpected. I thought we had at least another twenty years of living and loving together.

David was fond of saying he looked forward to caring for me when I got old. I think he would have done a great job. When I fell down the stairs of our house and had to rest for a week, he delighted in preparing tea and fixing meals for me. He was wonderful.

Although David will not be here to care for me when I am old, he found a way to make good on his promise. David was a big proponent of life, disability and long-term care insurance. We carried all of these types of policies.

When I retired from my job at the university, we realized we were putting all our eggs in the basket of our business. Though we paid off every debt but our mortgage, we still had monthly living expenses. We were banking on the business to provide the majority of our income for another six years.

Now I am leading and managing our business. Fortunately, I had learned the skills I needed. But that was not the scenario we had envisioned. The loss of David's leadership in our business added risk we had not anticipated when I left behind our other source of income.

I believe our business will go forward in strength, but no matter what happens, my income for the next several years is assured with the help of David's life insurance. After that, our retirement savings and Social Security benefits will kick in. David fulfilled his promise to care for me.

How about you? Do you have life insurance? According to the nonprofit Life Happens, more than 40 percent of Americans do not. Yet 70 percent of U.S. households with children younger than 18 would have trouble meeting everyday living expenses within a few months if a primary wage earner were to die, (LIMRA Household Trends in U.S. Life Insurance Ownership, 2010). And, the poverty rate for widows older than 65 in the United States is three to four times higher than it is for married women of the same age (Social Security Administration).

During his lifetime, David made a positive impact on the lives of hundreds, or more likely thousands, of people. My wish is that his positive impact on people's lives continue. May David's example inspire you to care for your wives, your husbands and your young children through the purchase of life insurance.

Key Takeaways

- Protect your loved ones from compounded trauma.

- Buy life insurance.

Epilogue

While I was writing this book, a friend asked me, "If you had to say what kind of movement you are trying to create with the book you are writing, what would it be?"

The question made me think.

Here is what I came up with: The movement I would like to create is a radical reframing of what financial success looks like.

If you construct your life so that you can live on less money than you make, you will reduce your stress and increase your wealth. You won't lie awake at night trying to figure out how to pay this month's bills. You will have the freedom to take calculated risks. And you will have the means to pursue interests and engage in activities that fill your life with joy and meaning.

That is what I call financial success.

Resources

These resources were where it all started for David and me. We liked to joke that we were absent that day in school when they taught financial responsibility. But in actuality, that day in school never came. My education about money began the day my friend mentioned that her son, a new driver, had damaged their car. She said no one was hurt and it was no big deal because she had an emergency fund. "What do you mean?" I asked. She told me that she had built an emergency fund based on advice in the book *The Total Money Makeover*. David and I purchased it and spent the weekend reading it together.

Below are my mini-reviews of several outstanding resources, including *The Total Money Makeover*, which helped us on our journey.

A Course in Prosperity: A 40-Day Manual for Masters of Prosperity by Julie Dankovich is a great resource to retrain your thoughts and erase old limiting beliefs about money. This book is very different from the usual "practical" resources for money management. Practical resources and actions can't produce the desired outcomes if they sit on top of negative beliefs. This book's 40-Day personal retooling program, intended to help you transform your beliefs about money, is a marvelous resource.

Embracing Uncertainty by Susan Jeffers was remarkably helpful to me during the transitional time in my university job when I didn't know who my boss was, on behalf of which medical departments I worked, what my responsibilities were or even whether I would continue to have a job. In one small example, the author lays out an exercise that moves the reader from a "hoping life" to "wondering life." Statements like "I hope I get the job" and "I hope he'll call" are changed to "I wonder if I'll get the job" and "I wonder if he'll call." A variation is waking up in the morning and saying to yourself, "I wonder what will happen in my life today." It's all about moving out of the victim's role and into the more empowering position of an adventurer or explorer.

the life-changing magic of tidying up by Marie Kondo was a useful guide when I was going through everything in my house to determine what to keep, sell, give and throw away. The author invites the reader to hold each object and ask whether it brings joy. If the answer is no, it's time to thank this object for its service and let it go.

Practicing the Power of Now by Eckhart Tolle is a gem. It's my go-to book when I am feeling stressed, frustrated or sad. It's full of quick, easy exercises that help me focus on this moment—the "now"—and feel gratitude for everything in my life.

I came across *The Smartest Investment Book You'll Ever Read* by Daniel R. Solin in a bookstore about a year after my husband and I took charge of our monthly budget and started telling our money what to do. I had realized that there was still one area of our finances in which I was acting like a scared child: our investments. This book helped empower me.

Solin's main point is that hyperactive investing doesn't make sense since nobody can time the stock market or consistently beat it. What makes sense, he says, is to invest in index funds, which hold all the stocks in specific segments of the market. An example is the S&P 500 Index Fund, which holds stock in the 500 widely held companies that make up that index. An index fund will always match the returns of the stocks in that segment of the market. Because index funds are not actively managed, their cost is low. That leaves more money in your account, which means you have a bigger base on which to earn compound interest.

Solin provides model portfolios made up of specific index funds at Fidelity, Vanguard and T. Rowe Price and provides a questionnaire for readers to use to determine how much of their portfolio they should invest in domestic stocks, international stocks, and bonds.

Shortly after reading this book, I met with our investment advisor and thanked him for his many years of service to us. We started investing our retirement assets as Solin recommended, and have never looked back. Incidentally, we moved all our retirement investments to Fidelity. For years, we met twice a year with a Fidelity representative to review our portfolio, make small modifications and ensure we were on track. Periodically, we used Solin's questionnaire to ensure we were appropriately balanced between stock and bond funds.

Start Late, Finish Rich by David Bach is a very practical book with section titles such as "Spend Less," "Save More" and "Make More." I especially like the part of this book that provides instruction about how to get credit card companies to lower your interest rate and waive fees. Bach implores the reader, "Do not—I repeat, do not—ever try to negotiate a lower rate with the first person who answers the phone." Bach has written a series of books with titles similar to this one. This is the only one I've read, but the rest look similarly helpful.

Stop Acting Rich by Thomas J. Stanley, author of *The Millionaire Next Door*, makes the point that if you live in a high-prestige neighborhood, you are likely to fall into the trap of spending a lot of money to keep up with your neighbors. Having a beautiful house, new car and luxurious furnishings will not make you rich. More likely, they will bring you debt and the stress which results from it. By making different choices about where and how you live, you can produce a different outcome.

Thinking Smarter by Shlomo Benartzi is a remarkable little book written by a man who was commissioned to study why people don't save more for retirement even when they have well-paying jobs and access to generous employer-matching programs. Benartzi, an expert in complexity theory, introduces a concept he calls a "thinking architecture." He guides the reader through this structured process of breaking down a problem into a series of manageable thinking steps. The book focuses on the problem of creating a fulfilling retirement. I found the Thinking Smarter structure to be easily adaptable to any complex problem.

When I left my employment at the university, I was grateful to have the opportunity for a "second act" and was determined to make the most of it. I used the Thinking Smarter structure to create three tiers of priorities for my time and attention. I periodically revisit and remodel my priorities. The book you are reading now is an outcome of my having used the Thinking Smarter process.

The Top 10 Distinctions Between Millionaires and the Middle Class by Keith Cameron Smith is a little book that makes several interesting points. The one most enlightening for me was that the primary goal of the middle class is comfort while the primary goal of the rich and very rich is freedom. This is why many in the middle-class abandon using a budget and working toward long-term financial goals. Because middle-class people value comfort over freedom, the author says, they don't persevere when the going gets tough. Middle-class people think month to month. Rich people think year to year. Very rich people think decade to decade.

The Total Money Makeover by Dave Ramsey lists seven "baby steps" to achieving financial peace. David and I were energized and excited by what we learned reading this book. We began to rough out our budget. We listed all our debts from smallest to largest. We started to formulate financial goals. Within a few weeks, we had built our first monthly budget. We began to see opportunities to change our spending habits and make progress toward our goals.

You Are a Badass by Jen Sincero is a crazy-fun book about how to get out of your own way and create a life you love.

Your Money or Your Life by Joe Dominguez and Vicki Robin is a classic work about our relationship with money. The authors propose that money is actually a measure of life energy. If you earn twenty dollars per hour in your job and you purchase a pair of boots for $100, you're trading five hours of your life energy for that pair of boots. The authors ask interesting questions that encourage readers to think more deeply about the value of their time and, ultimately, their lives.

76

Appendix A
Financial Goals Chart

See charts on the following page.

1. List your top priority financial goals in the order in which you want to achieve them.

2. Create target dates for achieving each goal.

3. Mark the date each goal is achieved.

4. Add, delete or edit goals as appropriate.

Financial Goals Chart

Example

		GOALS	TARGET	COMPLETED
DONE	#1	Pay off VISA		1/30/09
DONE	#2	Build emergency fund to $2,000		2/14/09
DONE	#3	Pay off AmEx 4.9%		7/31/09
	#4	Pay off AmEx 3.9%	12/31/09	
	#5	Save: $6,000 Used Car	6/30/10	
	#6	Emergency Fund to $5,000	12/31/10	

Yours

		GOALS	TARGET	COMPLETED
	#1			
	#2			
	#3			
	#4			
	#5			
	#6			

Appendix B

Monthly Budget Worksheet

See charts on the following pages.

1. At the beginning of each month, complete the "Budget" column for monthly expenses and income.

2. Use the mini-charts to help you predict and track your spending in the "variable" categories throughout the month.

3. Every few days, or at least once a week, update your "Spent Month to Date" and "Balance for this month" columns.

4. Change the chart and mini-chart categories to ones that work for you.

5. Use a budget every month to help you take charge of your money and achieve your financial goals.

Monthly Expenses

Category	Budget	Spent month to date	Balance for this month
Mortgage/ Rent			
Utilities			
House Maintenance			
Groceries			
Insurance			
Education			
Transpo			
Med/Hlth			
Clothing			
Recreation			
Personal			
Charity			
Debt Paydown			
TOTAL	$	$	$

Monthly Income

Source	Budget	Received month to date	Balance due this month
Salary #1			
Salary #2			
Other Income source			
Other Income source			
Other Income source			
TOTAL	$	$	$

Budget Mini-Charts

Utilities

total $

House
Maintenance

total $

Education

total $

Medical

total $

Groceries

total $

Transportation

total $

Budget Mini-Charts

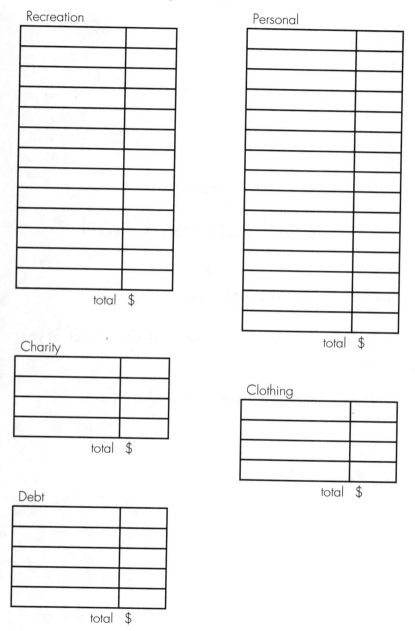

Recreation

total $

Personal

total $

Charity

total $

Clothing

total $

Debt

total $

Appendix C
Debt Progress Chart

See charts on the following page.

1. List the name, interest rate, and balance of each of your debts.

2. Each month, update the balance of each debt.

Debt Progress Chart

Example

Interest Rate	Debt	8/6/2008	9/6/2008	10/6/2008	11/6/2008	12/6/2008	1/6/2009
8.90%	Visa	$8,668	$2,984	$2,268	$795	$675	$550
4.99%	AmEx	$4,200	$4,122	$4,057	$3,932	$3,875	$3,867
3.97%	AmEx	$4,900	$4,989	$4,816	$4,730	$4,657	$4,579
7.15%	Equity Line	$39,772	$39,429	$39,083	$38,378	$38,018	$38,018
TOTAL DEBT		$93,230	$87,094	$85,554	$82,925	$82,195	$81,984

Yours

Interest Rate	Debt	Date	Date	Date	Date	Date	Date
TOTAL DEBT		$	$	$	$	$	$

Appendix D

Insurance Sinking Fund Worksheet

See charts on the following page.

1. Fill in your insurance premiums in the months in which they are due.

2. Add up the premiums in each row and write the total from that row in the final column.

3. Add up the totals in the final column and write the number at the base of the final column.

4. Divide the the number at the base of the final column by twelve.

5. The resulting number is the amount of money for you to save each month for insurance premiums.

Insurance Sinking Fund Worksheet

Example

Type	J	F	M	A	M	J	J	A	S	O	N	D	Total
Car Insurance			556						556				$1,112
Life Policy					278						278		$556
Disability				139						139			$278
Total													$1,946

Save per month: $162

Yours

Type	J	F	M	A	M	J	J	A	S	O	N	D	Total
Car Insurance													
Life Policy													
Disability													
Other Insurance													
Total													

Save per month:

Appendix E

Savings Progress Chart

See charts on the following page.

1. List each of your savings funds.

2. Each month, update the balance in each fund.

Savings Progress Chart

Example

TYPE	2/1/09	3/1/09	4/1/09	5/1/09	6/1/09	7/1/09	8/1/09
Emergency Fund	$3,167	$3,604	$3,036	$2,602	$2,602	$2,302	$7,224
Tax Savings	$200	$200	$875	$1,634	$2,384	$3,184	$3,984
TOTAL	$3,367	$3,804	$3,911	$4,236	$4,986	$5,486	$11,208

Yours

TYPE	Date	Date	Date	Date	Date	Date	Date
TOTAL							

Money Mindfulness, LLC
Ellen Abramson

Coaching, Consulting, Workshops

Money Mindfulness is my consulting practice. I help people create short- and long-term financial goals and a plan to achieve them. Because a monthly budget is the foundation for achieving financial goals, I work with clients to build personalized budgets to empower their spending, saving and giving.

For groups, I offer workshops and presentations on money mindfulness, financial goals and powerfully creating your financial future.

To explore how we might work together, please contact me at ellen@newmoneyfuture.com.

About the Author

Photo by Rose Massey

Ellen Abramson is living her "second act". After a thirty-year career in fundraising for the University of Michigan and the American Red Cross, Ellen carried out a plan to transition from full-time work for a large institution to a life in which she is in charge of her time and able to focus on what gives her life joy and meaning.

To make this possible, Ellen and her husband paid off $60,000 of loans and credit card debt and shed $23,000 of vehicle debt within a five-year period. She and her family live debt-free, empowered by a monthly plan for saving, spending and giving.

Ellen holds a Bachelor of Arts degree from the University of Chicago and Master of Social Work degree from the University of Michigan. She is president of NorthCoast Banners, and Money Mindfulness, LLC.